Listening to God – Fuel for Ministry?

An examination of the influence of Prayer and Meditation, including the use of *Lectio Divina*, in Christian Ministry

Listening to God – Fuel for Ministry?

An examination of the influence of Prayer and
Meditation, including the use of *Lectio Divina*,
in Christian Ministry

John Draper

Winchester, UK
Washington, USA

First published by Circle Books, 2016
Circle Books is an imprint of John Hunt Publishing Ltd., Laurel House, Station Approach,
Alresford, Hants, SO24 9JH, UK
office1@jhpbooks.net
www.johnhuntpublishing.com
www.circle-books.com

For distributor details and how to order please visit the 'Ordering' section on our website.

Text copyright: John Draper 2015

ISBN: 978 1 78535 448 9
Library of Congress Control Number: 2016934231

A CIP catalogue record for this book is available from the British Library.

Design: Lee Nash

Printed in the USA by Edwards Brothers Malloy

We operate a distinctive and ethical publishing philosophy in all
areas of our business, from our global network of authors to
production and worldwide distribution.

CONTENTS

Preface

Seen from the angle on an Anglican parish priest, this is a call to return to the base values of vocation; which is to pray and intercede for others as we listen to God through careful reading of scripture. The ancient monastic craft of *Lectio Divina* is seen as a window through which God can be heard and understood and in which there should be a context for ministry. This book examines how Monastic spirituality is seen as a basis for parish ministry as well, using as it does the gifts of God in ministry and through an intellectual approach to study. Making time to pray in silence is seen as a major element in this, there being a need to deliberately and regularly set aside part of the day. Just as listening to one another is important; so listening to God has to be an important part of one's life and ministry. The rise in the monastic movement, peaking in the Middle Ages, has interested Christians today, who are re-visiting the life of community alongside or separate from the mainstream Churches. This book asserts that a regular life pattern is necessary in those circumstances, as it is in parish ministry. Being an Oblate of a religious house can strengthen the spiritual life of both oblate and monks or nuns alike. Mutual prayer, support and spiritual guidance are available from this extended family. Seeking wisdom brings us to God, who is Wisdom and who is Love. Wisdom in oneself is acquired through the Holy Spirit working in us through the word of God and also through seeing God in other people. This is written in the hope that those who have moved from this disciplined approach to parish ministry may find that it will be enhanced if they follow this method and that they will be changed and their ministry will be transformed and invigorated.

To Hazel,
who listens to God with me

Acknowledgements

The Parish of St Mary the Virgin, Rowner and the Deanery of Gosport, who allowed their Rector and Area Dean space away from the 'day job'.

The Abbot and Community of Alton Abbey (Order of St Benedict) in Hampshire, who provided regular hospitality to dialogue, read, write, rest and pray.

My family, who tolerated my many absences and time locked away in my study.

Introduction

I am a priest in the Church of England, serving a large urban outer estate parish in Hampshire. I was ordained in 1990 and have come to value silence as a tool for re-energising my ministry. During specific periods of silence, which I aim to have on a twice-daily basis, I contemplate my ministry and pastoral contact with people. Often being asked to 'Say one for me, Father', I pray regularly for people and their situations and seek, in humility, guidance from God as to how I can deal with them. Amongst the busy and hectic activity of the day, I find it essential to take discrete 'time out' to be with God and to find my level of communication with God.

The prophet Zechariah [2:13] commands us to 'Be Silent, all people, before the Lord; for he has roused himself from his holy dwelling.' The discipline I follow is to have a half-hour period of silence in church before joining with others in the saying of the Daily Offices of Morning and Evening Prayer. Those Offices have times of general intercessory prayer, but in many situations I cannot bring the needs (many of them told to me in confidence) to public hearing. I may use a short passage of Scripture or a verse from the Psalms to meditate upon in total silence.

During silence, I often feel that God gives me a strengthening word of encouragement or advice, which I can then use to help others. I prefer total silence, without any sound (including music) for my contemplation. I want to explore why such silence which we might want to call 'attentive, prayerful silence', is important in the Christian tradition and usage; and what it is that we speak of when we talk about *this* silence. I know that silence is vital for me, but silences have been used down the generations of all religious followers in connection to prayer.

I will look at the Anglican tradition as well as the Roman Catholic and Quaker traditions. Each can teach the other through a selection of best practice. Prayer and contemplation in a mental, inner way, is for me a purposeful silence, a means to an end, with an intention: to listen to God. One can work in silence, read in silence, pray in silence and live in silence. For me, it is closely connected to a practice of spiritual reading known as *Lectio Divina*.

Lectio Divina is a craft based on 'hearing' God's word first, either through private reading or public reading during the liturgy of the mass or at the Offices; the individual then uses time throughout the day to return to a chosen text and hear what God is saying. So, I will also consider how such reading is treated by various philosophers and religious. I will also examine various writings on the skill of listening, which I see as a vital part of the previous two categories of spiritual silence and reading. All these things can be categorised as 'Spiritual Exercises.' I will begin with a discussion of various opinions and writings that tell us about the skill of *Lectio Divina*. I will also look at the way in which silence in the Christian tradition intersects with reading and listening in prayer.

I also wish to reinforce the view that our spirituality is not just about the trappings and functions of the office we hold, in particular that of a priest. Who we are is just one part; but our relationship with God, our fellow humans and the created world, is also an important part of our identity. I will examine what is the requirement of the office of priest in terms of public prayer and intercession, but will do so to emphasise the contention that the life of the Christian priest and layperson is one of relationship with Christ and the world.

I have carried out an extensive exegesis of various writings on methods of prayer, including the Benedictine disciplines, which include *Lectio Divina*. Although the use of *Lectio Divina* is important to me, I need to record some experiences of others, so I have had a series of brief conversations with members of a community of Benedictine monks, Alton Abbey in Hampshire. I myself am an Oblate or 'Associate' of that house and I have asked other Oblates of that community for their thoughts.

Much of what I have found in my own practice and those of other Oblates (of Alton Abbey) resonates with the writings of the French philosopher Pierre Hadot (a former priest, turned academic). I have been fascinated and gripped by his return to the disciplines of the Platonist and Neo-Platonists' Schools of thought, which offer us new insight into the silences perpetuated by two Medieval theologians, Bernard of Clairvaux and Hugh of St Victor, who I shall examine in the course of this book. In each case and also where I examine other writers, my focus is on the method and use of *Lectio Divina*, in past centuries by theological academics as well as those in ministry today. In each case the common thread that holds this thesis together is the value placed on silence and what is intended by this notion.

My *thesis* is that the parish priest's ministry can only be enhanced by following this method of prayer; and that her/his life will show signs of much change, following the expectation that Scripture will 'convert' us; in other words, bring about change and show difference. I spend some time on 'inner conversion' and 'conversion of life' generally.

All schools of religious thought concur on the need for the inner conversion of the individual through their life of reading and prayer. The whole Church can be transformed through further use of silence and contemplation. It is my contention that the whole company of heaven intercedes for us when we are praying as Christians, either individually, or as a group of people; congregation or religious community. Indeed, the writer to the Hebrews in the New Testament [12:1] tells us that 'we are surrounded by so great a cloud of witnesses.' St Paul affirms to the church in Rome [8:34] that it is 'Christ Jesus, who died, yes, was raised, who is at the right hand of God, who indeed intercedes for us.'

One of the things in which I have been interested, is whether

Lectio Divina is a practice best confined to individuals or to whole monastic communities or faith communities, such as a church parish. Is it something which only the parish priest is expected to carry out, or can it be shared by the congregation members? If there are ministerial colleagues, it is certainly feasible for this to be done within that group. For me, it informs my own listening and times of silence in specific times of prayer, as well as being a vein throughout my whole prayer life.

I will emphasise why I believe that the discipline is of use to the modern Church and argue that the re-introduction of formal spaces of silence and meditation into the lives of those in ministry will refresh the churches and give proper focus to pastoral and teaching ministry. The 'alternative lifestyle' of the monastery can be transferred to parish life, as we seek to bring Christ into the lives of the people whom we serve. There has to be a genuine and heartfelt will to pray the Offices and not merely say or read them, calling for a deeper pastoral slant to our individual and corporate spirituality.

This work is about the use and role of *Lectio Divina* in my daily life, which I try to extend into my public ministry in the Church of England and which I teach as a worthwhile method of contemplative prayer. It majors on that, but also on the equipment and tools which are necessary for a positive outcome: active reading, relaxed silence and focused meditation and contemplation. It goes some way to show that these things all propound the aim of the inner conversion of the soul and to the achievement of wisdom, which is knowing God.

Chapter One

The Origins and History of *Lectio Divina*

Introduction to spiritual reading

I wish now to introduce the method of prayer through reading known as *Lectio Divina*. The literal meaning of *Lectio Divina* is 'divine reading' and it is usually associated with prayer and the spiritual life. It is a prayerful study of scripture. Ann Matter describes it as a 'system of meditation on passages in the Bible, sometimes extended to texts based on biblical passages and redolent of biblical language.'[1] When applied to monastic practice, it is 'centred on spiritual experience, especially the arousal of compunction, the desire for heaven.' In monastic practice, particularly and in cathedrals' daily worship, the reading or singing through the Psalter with its 150 psalms, is an important part of this hearing and praying based on God's word.

Charles Dumont has written a pamphlet *Praying the Word of God* which is a précis of its history and application down the centuries.[2] In it, he quotes what is possibly the first ever mention of this method of prayer, in the year 256, in a letter between St Cyprian of Carthage and Donatus. This 'divine' or 'holy reading' is an ancient method of praying, using the Scriptures as an insight into God's will and plan for us.

Holy Reading, according to the philosopher Pierre Hadot, is a spiritual exercise, a way of life for some as part of their spiritual journey and discipline.[3] For Ann Matter says that it has been the influence and impetus for centuries of biblical study and scholarship, as well as prayer.[4] It is 'a method by which reading and interior exploration of scripture can open the soul to the possibility of union with God.'

Michael Casey helps us through the writings of Henri de Lubac and briefly explains his "four senses" of Scripture.[5] They are: (a) the literal sense; (b) the Christological sense; (c) the behavioural sense and (d) the mystical sense. These also tie in very well to the four 'moments' of *Lectio Divina*.

Casey paraphrases the meanings of the senses. The Literal sense is used by the intellect, is for understanding the text and is the first stage, *lectio*. The Christological sense accesses the memory and places the meaning in context, using stage two, *meditatio*. The behavioural sense applies the conscience, which lives the meaning through prayer, *oratio*. The last sense, the mystical, accesses our spirit, through which we finally meet God in the text and we apply *contemplatio*. The term was taken up by, amongst others, Saints Ambrose, Jerome and Augustine and thereafter continuously in the Middle Ages: It was Ambrose who said 'You are to be diligent in prayer and in *lectio*; that is how you speak to God and God in turn speaks to you.'

Dumont picks up that *lectio*, the reading, is 'actually and supremely the word of God for the praying soul. So the meaning of *Lectio Divina* is this: a word which comes from the mouth of God.'[6] I will argue in a subsequent chapter that silent prayer can be an active agent in this reception of God's word to the person engaged in contemplation and meditation.

Ann Matter tells us that, for her, the most useful biblical text for prayerful contemplation is the *Song of Songs*.[7] These are eight love poems in the Hebrew Bible (the Old Testament), which are allegorical writings about the love between God and Israel and have been traditionally regarded as helpful texts for contemplation. The writing is in stanzas, which makes for ease of meditation and contemplation of shorter passages and phrases. St Bernard of Clairvaux wrote eighty-six sermons on the *Song of Songs*, which Matter describes as 'short, fervent lessons of the spiritual life based in the text.' They were written originally for Cistercian novices of Clairvaux and speak of the many paradoxes and consequent tensions of the monastic life.

These examples show us that study of the biblical texts is as important as praying on them, so we should use some sort of preparation for prayer such as a commentary. Many Commentaries have been written by scholars and are in common use by academics and those in ministry, especially those with a ministry of preaching or teaching. On a simpler level, daily reading notes are available from the Bible mission societies to guide the reader towards discernment of a text and some suggest a focus for prayer or contemplation.

Benedict's *Rule*

Monastic life started out, first in the deserts and then either in the countryside or in urban settings. Originally, the communities were of pious laypeople. Mary Carruthers tells us that: [Monasticism was] 'not clergy [monks were not ordinarily priests until late in the Middle Ages, and nuns [women] were not ordained at that time] and as a particular way of living to be adopted only as an adult.'[8] I referred to monasticism as an 'alternative lifestyle' in my introduction and St Benedict was never far removed from the ideals of the early desert followers. In his introduction to Rowan Williams' book *Silence and Honey Cakes*, Dom Laurence Freeman OSB[9] writes of Benedict's rationale for religious communities:

> For him the ideal of the desert fathers was never far from sight. Externally this might mean that after years in the monastery the monk would move into a form of solitude. Interiorly it should mean that prayer becomes 'pure'.

Once monasteries became established, it was necessary for there to be some sort of regulation and many adopted *The Rule of Saint Benedict*; this builds on the *Rule of the Master* of Cassian and contains a whole set of guidelines for monastic living and is described as a 'Tool for Christian Living.'[10] Tomaine sets out for us the tenets of the *Rule,* including telling us of the instructions regarding the Prayer of Scripture (*Lectio Divina*), Stability, Obedience and Conversion of Life. Other foundations are hospitality, prayer and labour. St Benedict clearly sets down from the beginning in his *Prologue*[11] what each brother was (and is, still) to do regarding listening to God:

> Listen carefully, my son, to the master's instructions, and attend to them with the ear of your heart. This is advice from a father who loves you; welcome it, and faithfully put it into practice.

As part of the prayer life taught to disciples of the way of Benedict and to monastics and religious living in community, the method known as '*Lectio Divina*' is practised. Benedict says in his *Rule* [RB4.55] that the members of the community must 'Listen readily to holy reading.' In some communities today, a special time of day is set aside for 'holy reading', praying through the word of God, which sets the 'theme' of the day's meditation and the spiritual accompaniment to the labour of the monk or religious.

The life of the monastic is to be in prayer continuously as part of the *Opus Dei*, the 'Work of God.' The continuous prayer is a constant meditation based on reading and collecting sacred texts. Mary Carruthers[12] tells us that this was originally called the "memory of God" (*mneme theou*) by the early desert monks. For her it:

> [...] recognizes the essential roles of emotion, imagination, and cognition within the activity of recollection. Closer to its meaning is our term 'cognition', the construction of thinking. Monastic meditation is the craft of making thoughts about God.

In her *St Benedict's Toolbox*, American priest Jane Tomaine[13] writes that the scriptures offer us the richness of Jesus.

Through the words of Scripture, God reaches out to strengthen, heal, teach, and challenge. Scripture shows us the way to live and how we're to relate to God and to one another. The sheer beauty of its poetry and expression is yet another gift of Scripture. It's no wonder that Benedict rooted the Rule so firmly in the Word of God. The beauty of *lectio divina* is that it offers the gift of Scripture as a way to unite us with God and to recognize that we are personally loved by God.

Glenn Hinson in his chapter on Baptist and Quaker Spirituality in *Christian Spirituality* tells us that it is a common Baptist practice to read a passage of scripture at mealtimes and then spend some time in silent meditation, listening to the message of God.[14] This is also a common monastic practice, although the public reading tends to be of a pious text or spiritual biography. Some orders do have continuous reading of the Bible at mealtimes.

One method for using *Lectio* is to first quieten oneself down (perhaps through a breathing exercise) then offer a prayer to the Holy Spirit asking to be open to the Word of God and open to the guidance of the Holy Spirit. Then follows a slow, reflective reading (can be aloud or in silence) of a few verses of either scripture or some other spiritual writing. There then follows a meditation on the words, considering carefully, thoughtfully and prayerfully, how the words speak to an event or feeling of today, in our own context and circumstances. Prayer then takes place, sharing our thoughts, doubts and responses with God, offering feelings to God. The final part in the process is to 'come out of prayer'; and then contemplate throughout the day on the verse(s), repeating them perhaps at regular intervals.

Sue Pickering, a New Zealand priest who has a busy ministry of being a spiritual director and soul guide,[15] outlines the four parts of the method of *Lectio Divina* and relates, in terms of spiritual direction, how the blocks that form *Lectio Divina* can help anyone in a given context:

Lectio:

'Reading' the event or contemporary image that has taken our attention, taking time to explore our initial response to the 'key moment'.

Meditatio:

Thinking, reflecting, exploring, making connections, for example with scripture, with what we know of God through our experience or through what we have been taught or seen in others, with our own situations including our questions, struggles and joys. We listen for the inner promptings of the Holy Spirit who knows what we need to be asking ourselves!

Oratio:

'Talking' to God about what we are discovering about God and about ourselves through this event/image/'key moment'; responding to God with our whole selves, our feelings and our imagination, our bodies and our minds.

Contemplatio:

Resting in the love of God, letting ourselves be open to the Love which waits to enfold us, consenting to the work of the Holy Spirit within us.

Pickering's 'angle' in this instance is very much from an individualistic reading, although her book does cover other methods. When we read scripture, or, say a passage of text written by the Early Mothers and Fathers of the Church, we often experience or feel a sense of familiarity with events that are going on in our daily lives. We might sometimes 'relate' to a particular story or reading. The passage might also 'speak' to us in how we can deal with an issue. Thus we engage with the Word of God. Through our meditation, we might even perhaps feel that a character from the past is empathising with our particular needs today. Her method might give the impression that it is the individual who is more important than God speaking through that person. It is a 'social science' experiential take on scripture, with which some may find difficulty, as the focus moves away from God and the guidance of the Spirit; to concentrate on how the individual can react independently of the word of God.

John M. Sweeney, an American layman,[16] has written how the use of *Lectio* has transformed his personal and prayer life. He is a person who rushes around in a busy life, juggling business and family life and trying to live a monastic pattern of prayer life through this. He states that as an Evangelical layman, the monastic, Catholic, ways of prayer life have made sense in his life. He has tried many things in his spiritual life, but none were able to allow the spirit and words of his prayer life to meet. 'It was in more monastic ways that I found my prayer home: praying the psalms in the Divine Office; *lectio divina* or spiritual reading during prayer.' He also began using beads to silently chart a course of repeated prayers; and the use of centring prayer twice a day for twenty minutes. Sweeney asked his Cistercian monk friend Fr Basil Pennington about using *Lectio*: "It seems too simple to be a spiritual practice". Fr Basil replied:

It's simple to comprehend, but not as simple to do faithfully. Attending to it faithfully means become a closer friend with Christ. *Lectio* is another way of conversing with Christ. That's a mighty thing – mighty simple yes, but mighty. You see? And in *lectio* you allow Christ, as it were... you shut you up to the point where you allow him to pick the topic, not you.

Fr Basil was reminding the reader that it is God who is in control of the situation and not the reader. This is in direct opposition to the view of Sue Pickering, for example, who believes that our experiences shape what God gives us. St Bernard of Clairvaux's Commentary *On the Song of Songs* [23:6.9] is a guide to the reading of Scripture.[17] Bernard writes:

> By your leave then we shall search the sacred scripture for
> these three things, the garden, the storeroom, the bedroom.
> The one who thirsts for God eagerly studies and meditates on
> the inspired word. Know that there we are certain to find the
> one for whom we thirst. Let the garden, then, represent the
> plain, unadorned historical sense of scripture, the storeroom
> its moral sense, and the bedroom the mystery of divine
> contemplation. For a start, I feel my comparison of scriptural
> history to a garden is not unwarranted, for in it we find
> persons of many virtues like fruitful trees in the garden of the
> Bridegroom, in the paradise of God. You may gather samples
> of their good deeds and good habits as you would apples
> from trees.

St Bernard uses a familiar metaphor of the garden and gardening,
used often by Jesus in his teaching (*e.g.* the Vine, the Vineyard,
Mustard Seeds), mirroring perhaps the scene of the first
temptation, the Garden of Eden. The word of God needs tending
and nurturing by the gardener (the reader), before the fruits of
the harvest are gleaned (good works). Bernard was clearly
writing in this vein, having meditated at length on the scripture
and was living and breathing the text. Bernard again:

> Spiritual vineyards signify spiritual men within whom all
> things are cultivated, all things are germinating, bearing fruit
> and bringing forth the spirit of salvation. What was said of the
> kingdom of God we can equally say of these vineyards of the
> Lord of hosts – that they are within us. We read in the gospel
> that the kingdom will be given to a people who will produce
> its fruits. Paul enumerates these: 'The fruits of the Spirit are
> love, joy, peace, patience, kindness, goodness, forbearance,
> gentleness, faithfulness, modesty, self-control, chastity.' These

fruits indicate our progress. They are pleasing to the Bridegroom because he takes care of us.

Henri Nouwen insists that we need spiritual reading, because there are so many distractions, so many issues facing us which need a spiritual response. When he walked down a street in his neighbourhood, he was bombarded on every side by consumerist advertisements, temptations to buy, read, try. He felt as though all these outside influences were trying to intrude on his inner peace and quiet through words and images, to lure him away from a life committed to God. He asks whether we wish our minds to be the receptacle for all that is dross in the world. He argues[18] that we should be seeking all things that are Christ-like:

> Do we want our mind to be filled with things that confuse us, excite us, depress us, arouse us, repulse us, or attract us whether we think it is good for us or not? Do we want to let others decide what enters into our mind and determines our thoughts and feelings?

Yet Pierre Hadot insists that we should keep all the events of the world (including the dross) before our eyes at all times; that we should see the events in the light of the fundamental rule that 'memorization' is important in that we can keep both scripture and events in a parallel. This is done in order that we can shun the inner feelings and dialogues that come to the fore in our prayer life. In our meditation we are, however, trying to 'make sense' of events.

Hadot goes on to invite us[19] to think that we are actually 'healing' the world's situation and events through our meditation, a form of *therapy* in its literal sense of inner or outer healing and wholeness. This is a very Platonic idea and is similar to some other meditation practices which were extant:

[...] the exercise of meditation is an attempt to control inner discourse, in an effort to render it coherent. The goal is to arrange it around a simple, universal principle: the distinction between what does and does not depend on us, or between freedom and nature. Whoever wishes to make progress strives, by means of dialogue with himself or with others, as well as by writing, to 'carry his reflections in due order' and finally to arrive at a complete transformation of his representation of the world, his inner climate, and his outer behaviour. These methods testify to a deep knowledge of the therapeutic powers of the world.

Conversion of life

Once there is a way towards wholeness and healing through transformation, the Christian contemplative can see that this is part of the continuous journey of change and conversion. It was not a new approach ever, but one which the Greek schools had promoted. Conversion is achieved through giving oneself to something or someone else, evidenced either through outward activity or through inner peace. Hadot[20] compares this method to Buddhist practices of the Far East. Yet, he concludes that there is no real similarity, because 'Greco-Roman philosophical meditation is not linked to a corporeal attitude but is purely rational, imaginative, or intuitive exercise.'

Mary Carruthers recognises meditation as a disciplined cognitive activity, only appreciated through the *silentium* or silence of the time, which is part of monastic rhetoric.[21] It involves the making of images within our minds, which we use for thinking and composing. She continues:

The emphasis upon the need for human beings to 'see' their thoughts in their minds as organized images, or 'pictures', and then to use these for further thinking, is a striking and continuous feature of medieval monastic rhetoric, with significant interest even for our own contemporary understanding of the role of images in thinking.

Meditation, for her is a *craft* of thinking. 'People use it to make things, such as interpretation and ideas, as well as buildings and prayers.' The techniques of memory are important,[22] for Carruthers a 'universal thinking machine', both the mill which grinds our own experiences and the windlass used in constructing new thoughts and constructs.

Conversion is about seeing something in a new light. Robert Davis Hughes tells us that the word 'conversion' is borrowed from the Latin, meaning 'to turn around.'[23] For a Christian, conversion is a gradual and on-going process: in John's Gospel [John 3], Jesus tells Nicodemus, who is a member of the Jewish ruling council, that '...no one can see the kingdom of God without being born of above' (v.3). Nicodemus is confused by this and fails to understand this concept of conversion. Jesus continues (vv 5-8):

> Very truly, I tell you, no one can enter the kingdom of God without being born of water and Spirit. What is born of the flesh is flesh, and what is born of the Spirit is spirit. Do not be astonished that I said to you, 'You must be born from above.' The wind blows where it comes from or where it goes. So it is with everyone who is born of the Spirit.

The Charismatic movement of the Church has been associated with 'being born again', a concept about which Jesus teaches. But, for every Christian, living the pilgrim journey is part of the daily and gradual conversion process to new life, the new relationship with Christ and a new level of Christian witness, a moving *from* a life of sin *to* a life of grace in God and in Christ. The gospels help us to understand that Jesus' teaching about conversion was through being 'born again' through water and the Spirit.

The American academic Robert Davis Hughes[24] has written of the importance that the holy scriptures play in the act of conversion, from a life of being outside the Christian sphere to a life of Christian discipleship.

The best place to begin is with the first sort of conversion, the one most people think about when the word is used. This is a call, abrupt or gradual, *from* a previous life now experienced as sinful and defective, empty and meaningless, or badly distorted by oppression or abuse, *to* a new life as a disciple of Jesus Christ. This call comes through a variety of ways, from private reading of Scripture, one-on-one evangelization, the public preaching and worship of the church, or simply being raised in the community of faith in the midst of struggle until at some point one chooses to claim that struggle as one's own.

A.J. Krailsheimer puts it another way:[25]

[....] a dramatic change in external behaviour is not the principal, or even necessary, result of conversion, but on the contrary new relationship with Christ... a vital change has taken place once this relationship with Christ becomes an experienced reality instead of a pious phrase.

Hundreds of years before all this, St Bernard of Clairvaux was preaching about conversion of the soul, the inner being of one's existence. It is through the holy scriptures that people hear about God and, acting upon it, desire to be one of God and to settle their lives upon following him. Bernard[26] preached this Sermon in 1140 in Paris, his text being 'No one can be converted to the Lord unless he is anticipated by the will of the Lord and unless his voice cries out interiorly.'

You have come, I believe, to hear the Word of God. I can see no other reason why you should rush here like this! I approve of this desire with all my heart, and I rejoice in your praiseworthy zeal. Blessed are those who are mindful of his laws, provided that they obey them [Ps. 103:18]; 'To do his will is to live' [Ps. 30:5]. And if you would like to know what his will is: It is that we should be converted. Hear what he himself says, 'It is not my will that the wicked should perish,' says the Lord, 'but rather that they should turn from their wickedness and live' [Ezek.18:23].

Bernard sees the necessity for the turning of the soul (*i.e.* conversion). He also preaches on Our Lord's teaching that unless we accept the teachings of God like little children, 'you will not enter the kingdom of heaven' [Matthew 18:3]. So, Bernard is teaching simplicity of faith, as well as the need for repentance, leading to forgiveness, leading through conversion to a new life in Christ. It is Christ who teaches that 'Blessed are the pure in heart' [Matthew 5:8].

Bernard was writing from his point of view as a professed Cistercian monk, who was seeking 'converts' to Christianity, especially those who were willing to enter the monastic or religious life. One of the essentials of the Benedictine monastic way of life (which also governs Cistercian life) is to be on a journey that will involve the three dimensions of Obedience, Stability and Conversion of Life. The journey only ends on one's death and is therefore on-going. In the community of an abbey, of course, each monk is seeking the same and so there will be many opportunities 'In Chapter' (*i.e.* together as a meeting, reflecting on the day gone and the *Rule*) to consider progress together.

Robert Davis Hughes writes:[27]

Conversion is never just a private matter. Nor is it the beginning of the journey, let alone the end: it is only the first signpost that tells us that the journey has actually begun. In that sense the journey of the spiritual life is like any ordinary journey in that it begins long before it "begins" and lasts long after it is over.

However, fellow American F. Bailey Gillespie does not quite agree,[28] as he believes that conversion is primarily a 'personal, private affair, and any attempt to model a generic type is fruitless.' This raises issues about the inner life itself. For him, too, there were many types and varieties of religious conversion, which must allow for genetics, environment, gender, tradition, personality. He writes further:

It is a personal experience because religious expression and belief is usually a personal affair. It is an attitude, since faith is an attitude of our whole person toward God and life in general. It is an integrative experience because it seems to involve all those factors in our personality which constitute us as whole.

I believe that the tension between personal and group conversion can be bridged. For some, it is a deeply meaningful and life-changing event; in fact, probably for all Christians who are aware of the presence of God. For communities, growing together in faith and belief is also the same, as they allow God to enter their collective soul. Whichever way on which we would agree, it will change outlook, experience, reflection and witness to the gospel. The focus will change from inward-looking existence to the opposite, which is always to be mindful of the gifts of the Holy Spirit.

Pierre Hadot, a philosopher by training, was well aware of how a spiritual conversion could alter somebody's personality and outlook. He feels that people need to alter their life to bring about full potential and even to feel fulfilled. He writes[29] that:

All schools agree that man, before his philosophical conversion, is in a state of unhappy disquiet. Consumed by worries, torn by passions, he does not live a genuine life, nor is he truly himself. All schools also agree that man can be delivered from this state. He can accede to genuine life, improve himself, transform himself, and attain a state of perfection. It is precisely for this that spiritual exercises are intended.

Chapter Two

Lectio Divina Today.
Is it Individualistic or Communal?

Monastic theology and spirituality

In this Chapter, I wish to research the ethos of the cloister, in other words, discover the roots of the theology which makes the life of the monastery unique. As a monastic Oblate myself, I will discuss whether the 'culture' of the cloister can be followed in the outside world, be it in homes or in parishes, or in new distinct religious communities. The life of service, prayer and study of scripture is not confined to religious houses, but obviously that is their prime aim. These disciplines, or exercises, happen in parish life too, so I wish to argue that they are not only valid, but an important aspect in daily life for a parish and its priest.

Monasteries/nunneries are communities of monks and nuns living together in a life of prayer, devotion and work. There is always an interesting interplay between the dynamics of the individual and the community as a whole. Many Western monastic houses had, by the 8th century, mainly adopted the *Rule of St Benedict* as its spinal governing document. St Benedict specifically deals with how the community should live together in toleration and respect. I have dealt with this in fuller detail in a previous chapter.

Dom Columba Stewart OSB (Order of St Benedict)[30] thinks that there is always a tension between individuals and the community and the *Rule* reflects Benedict's knowledge of that possibility as he speaks concerning the spiritual development of both. Stewart tells us that much of the first part is concerned with the individual's behaviour and responsibilities, before moving on to the life within the community and its leadership and focus. The Emperor Charlemagne (c. 742-814) had dictated that all religious houses in his domain should follow this *Rule*. This, in the Holy Roman Empire, achieved a unity in terms of liturgy and holy living and gave a common cause and ethos in religious houses. There was a political end: that of bringing stability to the unifying states of the Empire.

Monks and nuns withdraw from the secular world, to live lives of prayer and service, with St Benedict actually naming his first house a 'School for Service.' Julie Kerr[31] writes that 'The monk's life was a spiritual journey directed towards salvation, which was to be attained through prayer, meditation and adherence to the *Rule of St Benedict* and the monastic way of life.' Religious [the collective noun for monks and nuns] were called to live lives of humility and the observance of stability. Kerr states that the life 'in community' was a 'training ground, the first steps on the road to perfection.'

A prolific writer on Monastic culture is Dom Jean Leclercq, OSB. The training ground and school for service element is reflected in the title of his major work on this, *The Love of Learning and the Desire for God.*[32] It discusses monastic learning and spirituality and the title itself sums up monastic theology. Leclercq begins his study by stating that, for him, two major groups of texts give us the backbone of monastic culture and spirituality: that of Benedict and of Gregory the Great. The first gave us the *Rule for Monks* and the second a biography of Benedict in his *Dialogues II*. Gregory's other great work, *The Book of Pastoral Rule*,[33] was also a hugely influential work in the formation of monastic living and theology.

According to Gregory, who wrote the only contemporary biography, Benedict came from a patrician family in Rome, with an expectation of receiving a good education in philosophy and rhetoric. He was used to being taught and studying hard, so when it came to the study of holy scripture, he would have expected his monks to do the same, spending time reading, contemplating, unravelling meaning and applying their learning to practical situations and moral decisions. His *Rule* was written after he had read other rules of the early Fathers of the Church, such as Cassian; he amalgamated and integrated others' writings into what he felt could be a good way of following Christ and serving a neighbour.

Leclercq writes that some saw Benedict's monastery as an academy of learning, rather than a house of prayer. 'In the *Rule* we can distinguish the two elements which we have seen in the life of St Benedict: the knowledge of letters and the search for God.'[34] Benedict assumes that those who come to the monastery can read, although there is room for those whose forte is labour and prayer, rather than reading and study. In the Middle Ages, the role of the monastery turned into places of sacred learning and they were, in many instances, the foundation blocks for the universities.

"Active" reading became the norm, during which there were processes of meditation and "rumination" on the sacred texts. Leclercq cites Peter the Venerable, often regarded as the Father of Monastic Culture in the Middle Ages, who regarded contemplation as 'Without resting, ruminating the sacred words.' The new way of combining reading, meditation and prayer was to become the major religious psychology and culture from then on in monastic life. In secular life, reading, meditation and philosophising (theorising or discussion on a point) was to be the equivalent form of learning in academic culture.

In his chapter [9] on Monastic Theology, Leclercq[35] tells us that it became something of a norm for monasteries to produce scholars who were carefully studying scripture and texts for the benefit of their brethren; as it met their needs, it became a "monastic theology." He tells us that within the monastery and outside in the schools set up by monks, '"the intelligence of faith" was being pursued and that all agreed that "holy simplicity is good, but holy knowledge is better."' So, Leclercq joined the succession of monastic leaders who have believed that the intellect contributes heavily to monastic theology, contributing much himself through his scholarship. Ann Matter[36] tells us that he believed that *Lectio Divina* was 'centred on spiritual experience, especially the arousal of compunction, the desire for heaven.'

New Monasticism and Fresh Expressions of Church

Within the Church of England and the Methodist Church in England, there is a movement to recognise and encourage Christian renewal. The Fresh Expressions initiative is a response to new ways of being Church, moving away from the traditional Sunday church-building based worship and fellowships which are the tradition of the Church of England. The leadership of the new community can be either from one of the denominations, or separate from it, although it might see itself as allied to it.

The Church of England brought out a report in 2004 called *Mission-shaped Church – church planting and fresh expressions of church in a changing context,*[37] which sought to theologise and advise on how local churches should not only encourage such initiatives, but recognise and pray for them. The new groups are many and diverse and are described as 'post-denominational' (p.43). Many groups sprung out of the new base communities started in the South American continent and are thus seen as part of a New Monasticism in the Church, where men and women live together in community, under a simple rule, seeking to serve the local poor and to live lives of simplicity with few or no personal possessions. This goes back right to the Early Church. Some of the communities are gathered together and some are dispersed in a wider fellowship.

The Fresh Expressions website[38] tells us that there is a similarity between communities under the New Monasticism label and there are parallels, drawn upon the traditional monastic houses and orders. Both follow lives of intention, have a regular prayer life, times of contemplation, emphasis on hospitality and practical engagement with the wider community (especially with the poor). What is important for the renewal movement is that there is reading, listening, silence and meditation; this is on a par with the traditional monastic orders and is seen as core values.

One such example of a new type of community is the Contemplative Fire organisation. On their website[39] they ask 'Have you been disillusioned or alienated by your experience of religion? Do you sense that there might be a spiritual vibrancy at the core of the Christian path?' This community seeks, through local and national networks, to 'celebrate the sacrament of the present moment in the beauty of nature, in contemplative liturgy and teaching.' Under the banner strap-line of 'Travelling Light, Dwelling Deep', the theology of the group is about finding links between 'being, knowing and doing', through prayer, study and action.

Another example is the Quiet Garden Movement,[40] which started in England in 1992, with a vision of having a network of pilgrim centres, together with 'a lattice work of prayer and hospitality, comfort for weariness, laughter for enlightenment, nurture for the quest.' The movement was started with students on a Contemplative Discipleship course, who felt ready to engage with the Christian gospels' contemplative dimension, eager to act on the "being" part of being a human being. It offers, through its various linked network of gardens here and abroad a ministry of hospitality and prayer.

Both the Contemplative Fire and the Quiet Garden movements are only two examples of prayer communities which are aiming to return to simple Christian basics of hospitality and prayer. Just as the monastic houses do this, these are less formal in nature and structure and offer a less rigid protocol and set of rules. Again, simplicity is the key word, as well as an assurance of prayer through silence and reading of the word of God.

I believe that New Monasticism can also include within its aegis the growing number of men and women who are becoming

Oblates or Companions of religious orders and houses. An act of oblation is a commitment, through vows and humility, to be associated with a particular house of an order and to keep it in regular intercessory prayer, with the assurance that there is a mutual activity of prayer for the Oblate or Associate. There might also be a commitment to keep the divine monastic offices (Morning Prayer, Midday Prayer, Evening Prayer, Night Prayer/ Compline) and to regularly attend mass and confession. There would also be a commitment to having a spiritual director/soul friend, who listens to the Oblate or Associate and talks to them about their prayer life.

An Oblate friend told me that, for him, this has become a spiritual oasis for him, as it releases him temporarily from the busy life which he leads as a computer consultant and a man with a young family. He is enabled to be and feel part of the monastic family whilst being away from it. Another has said that when he has a particularly difficult situation, he will pick a favourite piece of scripture (sometimes from the Psalms) and meditate for a 'good time' (possibly overnight) and respond, having found peace amongst the words of God. For some, it is a regular part of the prayer-time before the morning Office, when the upcoming events of the day will be offered to God. Oblates are taught this and commit to attend a Retreat where further coaching is given.

Another Oblate friend has said that he lists each event that is definitely happening and lays it at the foot of the cross, which will call down holiness and blessing upon it. One other has said that it is best not to meditate too late at night, or when particularly tired, for fear of sleep taking over his thoughts. Bringing all those with whom he has come into contact during the day and placing them in the context of the servant ministry of Martha, helps a friend remember that he is called to serve his people in the parish. All of them depend heavily on the prayer of all the Oblates and monks each day as they are named in a rotation of prayer intention. This allies them spiritually to their monastic home. Most have 'escaped' to the monastery for time away from their normal duties to refresh or to seek spiritual guidance, many of the monks acting as spiritual guides or directors.

Rachel Srubas, an Oblate of an American Benedictine nunnery, writes that, for her, perhaps the most important part of her oblation is the keeping rigidly to the rule of Prayerful Reading, Prayerful Writing.[41] She says that:

> Many contemporary people of faith are drawn to Benedict because his teachings not only offer an antidote to the culture of overwork, they also promote an approach to sacred reading that engages the whole person, and not only the rational intellect.

She tells us that there is a growing number of Christians in North America who are interested in adding to and strengthening their life of faith through the practice of *Lectio Divina*. She knows of many groups which are springing up to do this together, rather than individually. Such groups might study and pray together in silence, but there is a growth in talking groups, which respond to the Holy Spirit and actually name practical intentions to perform in the ensuing period.

Following St Benedict's *Rule*, there is a growth in oblation because people are drawn to the facets of conversion and stability, two major tenets in Benedictine monastic spirituality, although it was a common practice before then. Chapter 59 of the *Rule* is about 'The Offering of Sons by Nobles or by the Poor.' This was an offering of a member of the family to ensure that, not only the Order would continue and thrive in future generations, but that gratitude to God was shown through sacrifice. The boys could grow up to be monks, or could take the option of leaving when reaching maturity. This tradition continued, in a way, right up to recent times, when families were encouraged to offer one of their own to be a priest or religious. Benedict writes:[42]

If a member of the nobility offers his son to God in the monastery, and the boy himself is too young, the parents draw up the document [...] then, at the presentation of the gifts, they wrap the document itself and the boy's hand in the altar cloth. That is how they offer him.

Nowadays, there is no compunction on anyone: either on the Oblate to apply, or the monastery to accept. An application is made because of an association that has built up over the years. Brother Benet Tvedten OSB[43] believes that being an Oblate is like having a love affair, in this case with a particular house or order. As monks and nuns profess vows, including stability, which hold them to their communities for their life, so an Oblate or Associate publicly states their solidarity to a particular house. Tvedten also quotes a 'Simple Guideline for Oblates' which were drawn up for Benedictines in 1971 by a group of spiritual directors. They are:

Oblates strive for their own continued Christian renewal and improvement.

Oblates strive to be men and women of practical spirituality.

Oblates strive to be men and women of prayer.

Oblates strive to be men and women of Christian virtue.

Oblates foster a spirit of community.

When we are listening to God, or studying scripture, or praying to God, I believe that we do so in company with the communion of saints. No Christian is in isolation, even though they might live the life of a hermit. No Oblate is in isolation, as they are associated with a religious house or order which will have its lectionary (programme of biblical readings) and cycle of prayer (for members of the community and oblates and associates). No member of a religious order or house can see what they do in isolation of their brothers and sisters in community.

Michael Casey[44] encourages the modern reader to do so again in the 'old' way, *i.e.* reading together, either corporately or individually in the same room. He thinks it is a good idea for families or groups to experiment with this in order to build a sense of community. This could be done by sharing a common prayer first or at the end of the reading session; there could be discussion and sharing of thoughts; there could be many texts or books used in the exercise.

Casey believes that sometimes it is worthwhile for there to be more support than has formerly occurred in 'private' reading, although he does not wish there to be constraints on the individuals to work in groups. Whichever method comes to be adopted, Casey wants it to be a channel of meeting with God.

Chapter Three

The Principles of Monasticism Revisited

The last Chapter dealt with the resurgence in interest in monastic spirituality and life. I have seen evidence that there is a high number of people of all ages exploring their vocation to the monastic life. Many people are also attracted to the 'fringe' expressions, as was explored in this section. They are searching for safe havens for their calling, where they can be valued and respected and also their stories heard attentively over a period of time.

I now seek to explore the basic and important tenets of monastic spirituality, but seek also to relate this to parish living and experience, remembering that it is about seeking God and acquiring wisdom.

Reading

An important thrust of my argument is that parochial clergy and their people need to return to basics when it comes to reading and studying the word of God. The purpose of the study is to understand more of what the meaning of the passages of texts is. The reason why there is a need to do this, is so that the call of God is heard clearer and a prayerful response is made.

The Bible is not just written text: it is the record of inspired living and contained words of prophecy from the ancient Fathers of Israel. It is also a record of Jesus' ministry and that of the Early Church. The present generation needs to be revitalised itself to reflect this in today's age. Silence appears to be taking a back seat in life in general, with so many noises and distractions around. Silence is an essential facet of meditation and contemplation. Mariano Magrassi writes:[45]

Meditation,[46] personal prayer, and mysticism spring from the Word found on the lips of the Church at prayer. [...]This traditional conviction has proved surprisingly fruitful. We urgently need to make it our own today. If the soul is conscious of its identity with the mystery of the Church, it will spontaneously rediscover the close link between liturgical hearing and personal meditation.

Reading is both a way of receiving and understanding text. In a way, reading is silent listening, in that we are being communicated with and we are receiving words of someone else. The process of reading starts with the eyes and then the words reach the brain, which carries out a 'transaction' with the reader. Alberto Manguel, in his *The History of Reading*,[47] tells us that Cicero called the eyes "The keenest of our senses," in that it is easier to remember a text from reading it, rather than hearing it. Manguel also tells us that the Greek physician Galen believed that, having come through the brain and the optic nerve, the words of a page flowed into the air. 'The air itself then became capable of perception, apprehending the qualities of the objects perceived however far away they might happen to be.'

Manguel informs us of St Augustine's view that it is both the heart and the brain which act as 'shepherd' of all the senses stored in our memory, both collected and summarised and that they are 'shepherded out of their old lairs, because there is no other place where they should have gone.' Hundreds of skills are used in reading and perception of any text: 'inference, judgement, memory, recognition, knowledge, experience, practice.' It would have been the norm to read aloud, but Manguel tells us[48] that St Augustine noted that St Ambrose started a new trend by reading silently:

When he read, his eyes scanned the page and his heart sought out the meaning, but his voice was silent and his tongue was still. Anyone could approach him freely and guests were not commonly announced, so that often, when we came to visit him, we found him reading like this in silence, for he never read aloud.

Memory is also important in reading. The ability to memorize text is central, for example, to the practice of *Lectio Divina*. Augustine was impressed by a school friend's ability to recite from memory. His friend could impress the texts 'on the wax tablets of memory.' Manguel[49] opines that 'by recalling a text, by bringing to mind a book once held in the hands, such a reader can *become* the book, from which he and others can read.' This would certainly have been true in the classical and medieval worlds.

Dom Jean Leclercq also held this ability in highest regard[50] as the ability to learn a text is co-terminus with meditating on a text 'since the mouth pronounced it, with the memory which fixes it, with the intelligence which understands its meaning and with the will which desires to put it into practice.' St Augustine, referred to earlier, held that memory is '…the whole mind' (from his *Confessions X*), 'it is potentially the whole spiritual world, for, to know anything is to have it in mind, to hold it in my memory.'[51] Ronald Teske tells us[52] that, for Augustine, 'memory is not a distinct power of any faculty, but the mind itself, from which memory, […] understanding, or will are distinguished only in terms of their different activities.'

Augustine writes in his *Confessions* X.viii:[53]

The power of memory is prodigious, my God. It is a vast, immeasurable sanctuary. Who can plumb its depths? And yet it is a faculty of my soul. Although it is part of my nature, I cannot understand all that I am. This means, then, that the mind is too narrow to contain itself entirely. But where is that part of it which it does not itself contain? Is it somewhere outside itself and not within it? How, then, can it be part of it, if it is not contained in it?

One reason we might read a text is to educate ourselves and to be ready to be 'transformed', or, using a major Christian word, to be 'transfigured'. Being transformed is being willing to take on another view and to change. Changing to be like Christ and being affected so much that we walk with Christ is known in theological terms as being 'Transfigured,' which is a change in our physical nature. This act of God and episode in the life of Jesus is, according to *The Encyclopedia of Catholicism*,[54] serves as a literary device 'to place Jesus on the same level as the Law and the Prophets. He is the authentic source of divine truth for those who would listen to him.'

Kenneth Stevenson, when talking of the Transfiguration of Jesus Christ, believes that it is both an *event* and a *process*.[55] Christ is transfigured, in the presence of Peter, James and John, and a voice from the cloud says [Matthew 17]: "This is my Son, the Beloved; with him I am well pleased; listen to him!" Having had the glory of God revealed to him, he is altered in character. Matthew's gospel tells us that 'his face shone like the sun, and his clothes became dazzling white.'

In the New Testament story of the Transfiguration of Christ, Moses and Elijah appear on his either side and the disciples see the glory of God revealed through them. It is part of their way to believing, part of their 'discipleship'. The disciples have come to know of the glory of Christ and have had the true meaning of his being revealed to them by the work of God in the Transfiguration. Stevenson links their true realisation of the Messiah-ship and divinity of Christ to their own personal journeys of faith. Just as Christ is changed through his Transfiguration, so the follower of Christ is changed, or confirmed through accepting him into her life. For Stevenson, this is not a 'spiritual luxury with a feel-good factor', but something which is fundamentally concerning the

Church's discipleship, which is Christ-centred.

The Christian who has achieved inner conversion (or is on the journey towards it) has achieved a change in their outlook and discipline as well as their love and treatment of their neighbour. The ability to see Christ in those whom we love is a paramount part of this change:

> It concerns the understandably human desire to stay and enjoy the heights of revelation and prolong them as much as possible, thereby turning them into a human construct [...] The sheer fact of God in Trinity, the Father in the voice, the Spirit in the cloud, manifesting the transfigured Christ, points to the essential distance between humankind and the deity – a distance breached by Jesus, to whom alone we must attend.[56]

The medieval writer Hugh of St Victor wrote (in Latin, the normal language of the Church) in 1128 on reading and knowledge, in his *Didascalion*, which translated from the Greek means "things scholastic".[57] For Hugh (p.7), the primary purpose of reading, was to acquire wisdom: 'Of all things to be sought, the first is wisdom'. The wisdom Hugh seeks is Christ himself: 'Learning, and specifically, reading, are both simply forms of a search for Christ the Remedy, Christ the Example and Form which fallen humanity, which has lost it, hopes to recover' (p.10). There is a tension here between the monastic learning of the cloister and the scholastic learning of the newly-founded university.

Hugh was a cloistered religious (as opposed to a monk) at the Abbey of St Victor in Paris (which had been founded in 1110). Beryl Smalley[58] tells us that the abbey followed a rule which he wrote known as the *vita regularis et canonica*, which was based upon that of St Augustine. Hugh's rule was supposed to reform the clergy of the cathedrals but the laity also took it to their hearts and new religious houses were founded for intellectuals.

Smalley tells us that 'a gulf had opened between monks and scholars, […] the scholar learns and teaches; the monk prays and "mourns".' Hugh gave a great deal of time to biblical study and this, for Smalley, was a revival of scholarship of scripture, which was necessary to gain full understanding of their meanings. Full understanding would lead towards a greater fund of knowledge upon which to meditate. Ian Wei has argued that Hugh was trying to draw these two paths back together and that Hugh was very much part of a movement which tried to see co-operation between the Church and the Academy.[59]

The 'reading' which St Hugh is centring on is an activity of the monastery, for which intelligence and a good memory is necessary, as the reading is an aural activity. The hearer is required to gain skills in concentration, study well and practice the art of memory, which will assist the end-product – which is good meditation. Whilst the reading occurs, the hearer "mumbles" away with the words, finding the passage upon which to meditate.

Hugh writes:

Meditation is sustained thought along planned lines [...] Meditation takes its start from reading, but is bound by none of the rules or precepts of reading. Meditation delights to range along open ground, where it fixes its free gaze upon the contemplation of truth, drawing together how these, now those causes or things, or now penetrating into profundities, leaving nothing doubtful, nothing obscure. The beginning of learning thus lies in reading but its consummation lies in meditation.

Hugh proposed that any student of Scripture should know about the contemporary sciences, in order that they could 'learn every-thing; you will find nothing superfluous.'[60] Doing this would enable the student to expound according to the senses. So, in order that might assist the monk in his *Lectio Divina*, there must be 'a special course of studies as a preliminary to the investigation of each sense.'

R.W. Southern tells us[61] that Hugh began his 'Preliminaries' by discussing the difference between undesirable and desirable knowledge. This was to combat some of the teachings of the developing universities. Desirable forms of knowledge consisted of 'self-knowledge and the knowledge of God, together with the branches of knowledge which are necessary for these two purposes.' Undesirable knowledge would include anything which satisfies a need through curiosity. For the Christian, it was common to be learning and meditating, knowing that the reader would be mindful of their sinfulness and fallen-ness. Hugh would then speak of the Bible's subject-matter, including its dealing with two areas of desirable knowledge: Creation and Re-Creation, *i.e.* Redemption after the Fall. It is very much, for Hugh, a returning to God's basic message and teachings.

Another Medieval theologian who has influenced the view of knowledge is Guigo II. Guigo II was a Carthusian monk (1140-1193) who elaborated on the Benedictine practice of *Lectio Divina*. He knew that monks yearned to climb the ladder into the heavens, so he wrote for his order *The Ladder of Monks*. In it, he uses the metaphor of a ladder with four rungs. One day, whilst occupied with manual labour, Guigo 'began to reflect on man's spiritual work, and suddenly four steps for the soul came into my reflection: reading, meditation, prayer, contemplation.' For Guigo,[62] this method of prayer was a ladder by which they were raised from earth to heaven. Reading is:

> careful study of Scripture, with the soul's attention; Meditation is the studious action of the mind to investigate hidden truth, led by one's own reason; Prayer is the heart's devoted attending to God, so that evil may be removed and

good may be obtained; Contemplation is the mind suspended – somehow elevated above itself – in God so that it tastes the joys of everlasting sweetness.

For many, the *Ladder* is still a basic text in the understanding of the method and practice of *Lectio Divina*. Ann Matter[63] tells us that it dates from around the same time as the sermons of Bernard of Clairvaux. Guigo has insights from the biblical story of the vision of Jacob [Genesis 28:12], which tells us of a vision of angels going up and down a ladder to God, taking prayers to heaven and then bringing back God's responses. Guigo tells us that Reading, or *Lectio,* is for the rumination on scripture rather like a cow chewing the cud.

Pierre Hadot believed that all of the spiritual exercises, spiritual reading included (see earlier), are carried out in an effort to remove oneself from the inward-looking journey. Again, like Hugh, Hadot would have been conscious of the multi-faceted nature of humanity, all of which was fallen, in the sense of being sinful. But Hadot revelled in the differences of both Church and world, which enables dialogue and much time spent philosophising:[64]

> [...] fundamentally, a return to the self [in which we find God], in which the self is liberated from the state of alienation into which it has been plagued by worries, passions, and desires. The 'self' liberated in this way is no longer merely our egoistic, passionate individuality: it is our moral person, open to universality and objectivity, and participating in universal nature of thought.

Reading, in a religious sense, is carried out in a Monastic way; in the world of the academy, it is done in an Academic way. Monastic Reading is of scriptures and can include the writings of the Mothers and Fathers of the Church (known as the 'Patristic writers'). In both circumstances, reading can be aloud or in silence, to an audience or to oneself.

To appreciate and understand passages, it is helpful and useful to spend time afterwards in thoughtful consideration and contemplation. For the academic, critical analysis takes place, either alone, in a group or with a colleague; for the monastic, spiritual meditation is carried out, mostly in silence, but sometimes with a Spiritual Director or Soul Friend or mentor. This element of being taught also brings in a vein of scholasticism.

Proclaiming the Word of the Lord

Holy Scripture is not just *read*: it is *proclaimed*.[65] Mariano Magrassi[66] writes that 'Liturgical proclamation is obviously the place and privileged means of contact with the sacred text. There the living and active Word is returned to me in all its fullness.' For Donald Cozzens, the whole ministry of a diocesan (*i.e.* not monastic) priest 'is a spirituality of proclamation.'[67] Cozzens, an American Roman Catholic priest says that through the formation and maturity of the priest '[he]has encountered the power of grace unfolding in the depths of his own life and the lives of his people.' Proclamation is about making the gospel alive to people of today.

To understand Scripture, it is necessary for a reader to spend time reading it and also to discover what commentators have said about it, in order that it may be brought to life today. The *Catechism of the Roman Catholic Church*[68] reiterates the Second Vatican Council's document *Dei Verbum* and states that it is necessary to have a diet of Scripture in order to seek Christ:

> The Church 'forcefully and specifically exhorts all the Christian faithful ... to learn 'the surpassing knowledge of Jesus Christ', by frequent reading of the divine Scriptures. 'Ignorance of the Scriptures is ignorance of Christ.'

The 17th Century Anglican divine, Jeremy Taylor, wrote in his *Holy Living*:[69]

Rules for Hearing or Reading the Word of God.
1. Set apart some portion of thy time, according to the opportunities of thy calling and necessary employment, for the reading of holy Scripture; and, if it be possible, every day read or hear some of it read: you are sure that book teaches all truth, commands all holiness, and promises all happiness.

When the words of Scripture are read or heard, they are either mere words of record, or they can be regarded as inspired by God, brought alive by the presence of Jesus Christ, not only in word, but in Spirit also. Magrassi says that 'It is not the material sound of the syllables [of the biblical reading] that is life-giving. The hearer must understand with an enlightened faith the meaning of the message God is conveying.'[70] In other words, the hearer's faith must have been expanded and enhanced by hearing the Word.

Sometimes this word is received or proclaimed as part of the Church's liturgy; at other times, it could be as part of personal or private devotion, part of our individual life of personal prayer and meditation. Magrassi goes on to say that 'Vital hearing requires loving, calm, reflective, personal poring over the text... It is not enough to eat; we must assimilate, or as the ancients would say "ruminate".

Public liturgy, in the Catholic tradition, might not always be the best time to reflect at length on holy Scripture or to meditate on any particular word or passage. Within the constraints of the time allotted for a liturgy, it may be too rushed for this to happen. It is up to the homilist or preacher to bring out any salient or important points from a passage: to bring the Word alive.

The listener's mind might feel rushed in this context. The times of silence during liturgy will probably be too short for lengthy reflection on texts and passages (unless, of course, it is a service of meditation, such as a Julian Group Meeting[71] or in a Holy Hour – meditating before the Blessed Sacrament of the Eucharist; or in a Quaker Meeting).

It is in our times of private or personal prayer and meditation that we can choose a word of a passage, or the Preacher or Conductor of a Quiet Day or Retreat may set one for contemplation. It is perhaps during the times of inner silence that a new meaning can come to a phrase, or an intention may arise. That is one of the uses of the system of reading known as *Lectio Divina* (see previous chapter).

Silence

In this section, I wish to explore some of the many facets of purposeful, prayerful silence which are experienced by Anglicans and by Quakers; the former is based on a monastic theology and a medieval notion, the latter on the Puritan notion that pure religion can lead to the truth about God.

Silence can be experienced in a variety of ways and is therefore very difficult to define rigidly. It could mean an absence of noise and speech; or being in isolation; thinking or praying quietly; our inner depth of quietness; stillness; absolute quiet (which some people find very awkward). It can be part of our spiritual make-up and how we connect with God. There is a general assumption that with many Christian traditions, including the Anglican one on which I will focus, that prayer lies at the heart of the role of a minister. Within the history of Anglican discussion of this is also an assumption that prayer may positively be silent – a notion extended by the Quakers.

William Bloom, an Anglican who has specialised in modern, holistic spirituality and has directed the St James's Church Alternatives Programmes in central London, refers to spirituality as our 'spiritual connection' and analyses how, down the ages, Christians have wanted to 'guide, manage and deepen moments of spiritual connection and awakening so that they do not just appear serendipitously or haphazardly.'[72] He has mentioned three strategies for reaching such spiritual moments: (a) hymns and music, (b) the appreciation of the natural world and (c) silence.

These, says Bloom, guide the spiritual experience or encounter and make it more powerful and, because it can last longer, the fruit of that encounter will linger within the soul. Repetition is important, for the heart awakens more and the unconscious is vitalised. He thinks that this will happen with a one-off 5 minutes' calm silence, but prefers a daily experience of silence (he recommends 20 minutes). According to Bloom, the experience will be enjoyable and so becomes a joy and not a burden. Religion should not be a 'stern and curtailing pleasure.'

Within the joy of silence, it is possible to contemplate the truth about the love of God and what it means for an individual Christian. This moves us from a philosophical or academic approach to religion into a personal relationship with God, having submitted and approached God in humility, as well as in a sense of awe and wonder. In Book 3 of *The Inner Life* (part of his *Imitation of Christ*), Thomas-à-Kempis[73] writes, in Chapter 2, that 'Truth Instructs us in Silence'. Christ responds:

My Son, hear my words. They are of surpassing sweetness, and excel all the learning of the philosophers and wise men of this world. My words are spirit and life, not to be weighed by man's understanding. They are not to be quoted for vain pleasure, but are to be heard in silence, and received with all humility and love.

In the busy daily round of parish or commercial life, with its frequent encounters with people, either one to one, or in meetings or gatherings, one can get caught up with business and 'lose the plot', which is to try and live a life of the mystic (a holy person involved in the work of God) (and not be a worrier) (gleaned from a conversation with Canon Keith Lamdin, a former Principal of Sarum College in Salisbury); to be the person who will pray on behalf of people. Eugene Peterson believes that pastors should be apocalyptic and should *pray*. 'Apocalyptic' means pertaining to revelation, so in his sense it is about the revelation of God, '...the uncovering of what was covered up so that we can see what is there.'[74]

Peterson says that 'St John's [the writer of the Book of Revelation in the Bible] pastoral vocation was worked out on his knees.' Prayer, contemplation and study of scripture, therefore, is an integral part of pastoral ministry. He continues:

He embraced the act of prayer as pivotal in his work, and then showed it as pivotal in everyone's work. Nothing a pastor does is different in kind from what all Christians do, but sometimes it is more focused, more visible. Prayer is the pivot action in the Christian community.

Silence helps us to escape from the general background of noise and cacophony that intrudes into our lives; it also encourages us to 'slow down' from the humdrum and busy-ness that modern life has become for many people. It is a form of isolation of oneself. Jesus knew the problem of this and very often Scriptures tell us that he escaped from the crowds, or rowed out into the lake, or escaped to the hills to pray. Often he was interrupted. We know from the gospels that on the night that he was arrested in Jerusalem, he went into the garden to pray through the night [Matthew 26:36]. Some of that night was spent in silent prayer; some in oral questions to God; some in conversation with his disciples.

It is easy to forget that prayer should be the core of our being. Priests are reminded at their ordinations that they are to be 'prayer-centred'. At my Ordination as a Priest (using the rites of the Church of England),[75] the bishop told the congregation that 'He [*sic*] is to lead his people in prayer and worship, to intercede for them, to bless them in the name of the Lord.' Each candidate for ordination was also asked whether they would be 'diligent in prayer'. Michael Ramsey tells us[76] that Jesus' disciples (of whom I and fellow ministers are successors) 'prayed *with* Jesus, *near* Jesus: and what a difference that made!'

Ramsey assumes that the priest will know exactly *how* to pray and *when* to pray. He is assuming that the background of each priest contains sufficient knowledge and skill to enable this to happen and also how to discern God speaking through prayer. To some, praying and discerning the word of God through the Holy Spirit seems to come with ease; to others, it is a trial and an unachievable aim.

A Christian leader who prayed regularly was Saint Paul. In his letter to the Philippians [1:3f] he wrote: 'I thank God every time I remember you, constantly praying with joy in every one of my prayers for all of you.' This was quoted by Cocksworth and Brown[77] as being the major *raison d'être* of a priest. They wrote:

> Whatever else people want of us as priests, they want us to pray for them. Equally, being a person of prayer is a priority that most clergy set for themselves, part of what they see as their vocation.

One of the spiritual classics of the 1950s in the Church of England was Bede Frost's *The Art of Mental Prayer*. He enunciates that the problems which some have with their prayer life[78] are contained within 'Three truths':

> Three truths in connection with mental prayer [by which he means silent contemplation] should be constantly kept in mind: (1) That the main object of our prayer is to get into personal contact with God Himself; to gain such a knowledge

of Divine realities as shall lead us to desire, love and seek them for their own sake. (2) That the means of our so getting in touch with God is through the Sacred Humanity of our Lord. 'No man cometh unto the Father but by me.' (3) The true test of the value of our prayer is not the ease with which we make it or the consolations we may experience, but the deepened realisation of our own nothingness, the increase of our love and desire for God, and of our obedience to the Divine Will, and the closer conformity of our exterior conduct with our interior life.

For Religious and Ministers of Religion, silence needs to be an essential and integral part of their very inner being and spirituality, and part of their personal life pattern and Church discipline and order. As Jesus would go into the hills to escape the crowds and his busy life, full of pressures from people; so it is very good for all of us if we are able to do that as well. There are opportunities to have a Quiet Day or a Retreat, away from the clergy house, perhaps in a monastery or other quiet place, but away from the distractions of telephone and visitors. Again, Ramsey[79] tells us that:

> Simon Peter finds Jesus a great while before day praying in a desert place. Jesus prays through the night before the appointment of the twelve. Jesus prays on the mountain where he was transfigured. He rejoices in the Holy Spirit, giving thanks for the reception of his message. He prays in the garden of Gethsemane. He prays during the hours on Calvary.

Those who are frightened or threatened by silence are very often people who are leading rushed and busy lives and do not wish to take time to be still and reflect. I have known parishioners who, rather than sit still and quietly before a service, will be making themselves busy, for example tidying books or leaflets. I have also known clergy who have said that they are 'too busy in the parish' to take time away to have their own times of reflection and contemplation.

The writer of the hymn 'Dear Lord and Father of mankind', John Whittier (1807-1892),[80] includes three verses which are important, as they talk, not only of Jesus' finding of God through his times of quietness, but of our need to find God through a similar experience. We are encouraged to allow quietness to enter our veins so that our strains and stresses will be removed and that our newly ordered lives will confess God's peace in the world.

O Sabbath rest by Galilee! O calm of hills above, where Jesus knelt to share with thee the silence of eternity, interpreted by love!

Drop thy still dews of quietness, till all our strivings cease; take from our souls the strain and stress, and let our ordered lives confess the beauty of thy peace.

Breathe through the heats of our desire thy coolness and thy balm; let sense be dumb, let flesh retire; speak through the earthquake, wind, and fire, O still small voice of calm!

A major contribution to silence and contemplation in the Church has been made by the Quaker movement, founded in England in the 17th Century, in a response to what they believed was corruption of God and his people in the Church of England. Quakerism relies on silence to hear the word of God, rather than through set forms of liturgy and through sermons. For Quakers, they rely not so much on the Bible, but on the Inner Light, which is a 'source of direct revelation, guidance, and power.'[81] The movement was established to revive ancient Christianity's experience of the Holy Spirit. They feel that the Spirit of God is still at work in everyone's heart and known by all who respond.

Two Quaker writers are J. Brent Bill and Robert Lawrence

Smith. Bill refers to silence as 'Sacramental Silence'.[82] Members of the Society of Friends (Quakers) see silence as an integral part of their worship and prayer life; it is about meeting God intimately, silence being a form of intimacy. It is like sitting quietly with a friend, saying nothing, just accepting their company as valuable for what it is. After their period of silence, members will together try and discern what God has been saying to them at that particular time.

It is asserted in Quaker teaching that reading in silence and listening to God in that space can bring a new slant on our guidance. For example, Bill refers to 'holy' silence, which is sacred or sacramental, in that it is a visible sign of God's love:

I let myself be guided into the deep waters of the soul [...] we believe that when our hearts, minds, and souls are still, and we wait expectantly in holy silence, that the presence of Christ comes among us [...] it offers a profound spiritual encounter for any woman or man hungry for a fresh way of connecting with God.

Of course, the love of silence is not restricted to Quakers, but they are especially grateful for it and mindful of its value. Smith regards silence as purgative and 'cleansing'.[83]

He continues:

Friends view silence as a highly accessible treasure; its benefits are unquestioned. The riches silence offers are available to anyone at any age and in any place. For some, the contemplative zone of silence is the morning shower, where every extraneous sound and thought is blotted out by the rush of water. For others, it is the solitary morning commute, with the steady drone of traffic outside. The key ingredient is not so much the total absence of noise as receptivity and access to the "still small voice within."

The stillness referred to above is really a feeling of peace and contentment and knowledge of the love of God. Finding God and quiet in our lives can be very difficult; for some it is anathema. Martin Laird[84] puts our resistance and ignorance down to the 'constant inner noise and chatter that creates and sustains the illusion of being separate from God, who, as St. Augustine reminds us, is already, "closer to me than I am to myself."' He continues and gives us a fresh angle on silence and its essence:

> If inner noise sustains this perceived alienation from our inmost selves, we shall feel perforce alienated from God. But this sense of alienation or separation is generated by blind and noisy ignorance that insinuates itself in the surface regions of our awareness. Our culture for the most part trains us to keep our attention riveted to this surface noise, which in turn maintains the illusion of God as a distant object for which we must seek as for something we are convinced we lack. One of the great mysteries of the contemplative path is the discovery that, when the veils of separation drop, we see that the God we have been seeking has already found us, knows us, and sustains us in being from all eternity.

But silence does not just refer to the amount of noise we do or don't make; it is about our interior silence, our depth of being. For him, the 'deeper our own interior silence, the more we take on its gracious ways of opening up the tight mind that clenches its teeth around what it wants and spits out what it doesn't want.'

Graham Turner[85] spent some time at Thomas Merton's monastery in Kentucky USA, Gethsenami, where the Trappist monks run a silent house of prayer. The house was full of notices, such as 'Silence beyond this point' and 'Silence is spoken here.' Turner felt oppressed by their frequency, feeling a slap in the face, or a stripping of basic faculties. Yet eventually he became to understand that communication can still exist in silence, so that the nature of the human relationship can be transformed by silence, even laid bare by its nature and existence. He continues:

> It [silence] leaves us puzzled, at first, as to how we should communicate with each other. It strips us of all the verbiage with which we habitually garland ourselves and leaves us, in a sense, naked. Thus exposed, we have to relate to other people just as we are. It brings us back, in some measure, to the core of ourselves.

Silence, then, makes us vulnerable and, in theological and spiritual terms, exposes us totally to God's Spirit without the guards which we set up around ourselves. Sometimes, simply stopping what we are doing is a contributory fact to hearing God as well. Being still can be part of silence, although the two are not bound to each other. Henri Nouwen asks a very simple, yet deep, question about our sometimes being unwilling to be still and to wait on God. It opens up all sorts of questions about personal resistance, insecurity, lack of inner quiet. He writes:[86]

> Why it is so difficult to be still and quiet and let God speak to me about the meaning of my life? Is it because I don't know God? Is it because I wonder if God really is there for me? Is it because I am afraid of God? Is it because everything else is more real for me than God? Is it because, deep down, I do not believe that God cares what happens?

Bishop David Bentley presents us with the paradox that we love silence, yet we spend more time seeking it than getting it.[87] He talks of our relationship with silence being awkward:

> It [Silence] attracts us, yet quickly eludes us. We protest loudly that all we want is a bit of peace and quiet, but when we get an unexpected hour of space, we quickly look for

something to fill it. Even in our churches we speak about the need for silence far more than we actually allow it. More than once I have caught myself taking longer over the introduction of a time of silence than over the actual silence itself!

Kenneth Leech, an Anglican priest and spiritual writer, believes that coming to terms with silence is a necessary element in our prayer life and in discovering who we are as individuals. Religious silence is, for him, prayer or an important component of it. We are required in our prayer life to withdraw from our daily tasks and to discipline our thought and concentration. This is an attentive sort of silence which, when incorporated into prayer, will bring out more. He continues:[88]

The practice of silence is [...] the discovery of one's own inner depths. For when one descends into the depths of one's spirit, there is a realization of the closeness of God, the ground of one's being, the depth in which our own soul stands.

Leech decries the modern absence of silence in the world and believes that training is necessary in the skill and its use; he classes it as an 'inner resource.' He recommends particularly the use of retreats, both for the conductor and the retreatant, a time of refreshment and recollection. He refers to them as a 'time of awakening, of new vision and a new zest,' For Leech, there is also no need for prayer groups to be full of speech and utterances.

In another book, *True Prayer*,[89] he writes that 'There is no reason why a prayer group should not be entirely silent [...] and a prayer group in which people seek to grow in silence together can help.' Earlier in the book, he had written that 'Creative silence is a necessary part of prayer. Pascal once commented that "most of man's troubles come from his not being able to sit quietly in his chamber."'

Having experienced both types of prayer group (including

silent Julian Meetings) and many thousand hours of liturgy, I have to come down on the side of the Quaker spiritual disciplines. The Catholic Anglican approach has its roots in monastic liturgy and prayer and is often very 'busy' and fussy. Sometimes I yearn for the total stillness of the liturgy of the Society of Friends, who waits on God silently, looking for the Inner Light.

Listening

Listening is an important discipline and a skill which is taught from a very early age. It is a basic skill necessary for survival. The definition of 'to listen', according to the *Shorter Oxford English Dictionary*[90] is: 'To hear attentively; to give ear to; to pay attention to.' Listening is a component of dialogue, conversation, understanding, education. It is the other part in the equation amongst equals, whom we value. Not listening causes others to be angry, frustrated, under-valued, sometimes eliciting an angry response of 'You're not *listening* to me'; or 'You're not *hearing* what I am saying' from those whom we offend. Those statements reveal frustration that the aggrieved feels that they are not respected or valued. Listening, therefore, is a basic skill which is refined by those involved in any relationship (this will include pastoral work and any form of counselling).

There are special courses in 'Listening Skills', teaching us to be aware, 'awake', 'conscious' of what people say to us. Although we all prefer it if we are heard properly and attention is paid to our needs and desires, it is not always mutual. We have to use the discipline of listening in our everyday lives. One of the leading teachers of Counselling Skills, Peter Sanders, has written that those helping people 'Observe, Understand and then Reflect.' He thinks that *active* listening is one of the crucial parts in a helping relationship.[91]

If, in Ministry, through our prayer life, we are trying to listen to God and, through other Christians, to understand what God is saying to others, perhaps Sanders' basic rule of thumb is necessary. For him, it is absolutely impossible to be helpful if we don't listen. His field is humanistic counselling, but his rules fit the Christian well:[92]

> Active listening means that you have to attend to all of the signals given off by a person... the purpose is to pay attention to, and try to understand, the thoughts, feelings of the other person.

Why does the Christian want to listen to God in the first place? The Christian will love God, so would pay attention to what God is saying, just as they would to a friend, or lover. They would stress that God's word can be inspirational, guiding, soothing, comforting, hallowing, affirming, transforming, awe-inspiring, terrifying. They would then ask, perhaps, how one could then apply Sanders' 3 key components of Listening (Observe, Understand, Reflect) to hearing God's word to us? How do we hear what God is saying (observing or noticing)? How do we begin to discern it (understand)? How do we reflect upon and act upon it through *praxis* (reflect)? *Lectio Divina*, a form of contemplation, is believed to help the believer do these three things and this is dealt with in greater depth in other chapters.

Lectio Divina is a conversation with God, which also depends of their being a great deal of silence. A conversation is two-sided; the best one is when we are balanced in our contributions, valuing each-other's participation of speaking and listening. Martin Smith says that 'Prayer is a conversation with God.'[93] And so it could also be said of our prayerful relationship with God, in that we speak and God listens; God speaks and we listen. Our relationship with God through Prayer helps us to listen to God; meditating on the Scriptures helps us to discern what God is saying to us today through his Word.

Dale Allison is confident that modelling prayer on conversation 'implies that, in addition to speaking, we refrain from speaking. One-sided conversations are not usually very rewarding, and our experience in this matter holds equally for prayer: our chatter needs to cease.'[94] He tells us of Eastern and Western methods for creating stillness:

> [...] that might allow the ears of the soul to hear the divine whisper. Whatever the means, the goal has been the same: to slow or stop the torrent of thoughts that ever floods our minds and keeps us from encountering what lies beyond, that being a place wherein speaking can defer to listening, wherein prayer can become not something that we do but something that we receive as we wait upon God in hope and faith.

What I bring to God, though, is current and active. It could be a situation on which I seek guidance; or a particular person who is struggling with an issue; it could be me, asking for assistance through a matter with which I have currently been grappling or struggling. Pierre Hadot wishes us always to have the events of the present with us when we are praying. For him, it is the key to spiritual exercises, for 'it frees us from the passions, which are always caused by the past or the future – two areas which do *not* depend on us.'[95]

Conclusion
Lectio Divina in Parish Life

Study and Prayer

The aim of this book has been to iterate and highlight the benefits of silence, focused reading (using the method of *Lectio Divina*), meditation and contemplation for all those who are involved in the Church's ministry. My own learning has been enhanced as has my appreciation of other traditions within the Christian Church. I have attempted to exhibit how Silent meditation and contemplation, especially the method and practice of *Lectio Divina*, are, for me, useful methods of disciplining my life of prayer and intercession in public ministry.

The progressive and steady study of the scriptures, using the readings of the day, is a time of invigoration and purposeful meditation. One of the definitions of 'study' is 'Thought or meditation directed to the accomplishment of a purpose.' This older, classical, definition of 'study' helps the modern-day parish priest focus on what intercessory prayer and focused reading are about: a meditative study of scripture and its practical, prayerful and pastoral application.

Silent meditation is more than escapism – well, for me, anyway. When I need inspiration or support from the God whom I believe made me and who strengthens me, the most natural response is to copy the psalmist, who in Psalm 121 [v.1f] wrote: 'I lift up my eyes to the hills – from where will my help come? My help comes from the Lord, who made heaven and earth.' This has been a constant source of meditation when I have been searching for a way forward in a pastoral or personal issue in my life as a Christian and as a priest. When really depressed, however, thinking that God has just switched off for a moment, I might turn to Psalm 22 [v.1]: 'My God, my God, why have you forsaken me? Why are you so far from helping me, from the words of my groaning?'

The advantage of silent meditation and of the use of *Lectio Divina*, is that one has to slow down in the high-speed world in which we live. Donald Cozzens,[96] writing as a Roman Catholic priest who trains others at seminary, says that those with whom he comes into contact are increasingly aware that some sort of silent, meditative prayer is vital to the life of the priest. 'When priests speak of their spiritual lives, more often than not they speak of a sacred time during the day when they enter into a period of solitude and wordless prayer.' For them, it is a time when they wait on the Lord, listen to God's spirit. During this time, they can discover what is going on in their own soul.

Cardinal Basil Hume, himself a professed Benedictine monk, knew that his diocesan clergy were not always faithful in prayer. He regretted that some had abandoned the saying of the Daily Office and spent little time in private prayer, using the argument that it was more fruitful to be carrying out the good works than thinking about it. Hume was quite clear where their priorities should lie:[97]

Although our priestly work will sanctify us as well as those to whom we minister, it will do so only in so far as we have an authentic spiritual life. We must make a daily effort to become more closely united to God. For this two things are essential: prayer and suffering.

An Anglican priest (and other denominations) is required to say the daily offices of Morning and Evening Prayer under the Canon Law (Church regulations) of the Church of England. Although promises have been by the ministers at their ordinations, *The Canons of the Church of England*[98] emphasise and attempt to enforce the saying of the Offices publicly, 'as may best serve to sustain the corporate spiritual life of the parish and pattern of life enjoined upon ministers.' So, as well as being an essential for the priest, it is a part of the rich spiritual and liturgical life of the Church.

Personal Transformation through prayer and meditation

Bishop John Pritchard[99] believes that the discipline of daily prayer works quietly through us, as 'it exposes us to scripture, psalms and spiritual songs (canticles) and it commits us to prayer as intercession.' It has another purpose, in that 'it wears away the rough edges of our character and aligns us to the character of God [...] its function is to carry us and steady us, to hold us in times of turbulence and speed us onwards in times of high pleasure.' He wondered, when he worked in a cathedral, whether he could live with the daily round of services, but found that they 'carried him along in a great river of praise [...] and my focus was re-directed towards God.'

Pritchard calls the Offices a bedrock. He emphasises that a priest needs to be spending time alone with God to help expand the relationship with God. 'Priests are in danger of heart trouble if they don't breathe deeply enough the Spirit of God.' He tells the story of a celebrated pianist who said that if he hadn't practised for a day, he would notice; for two days, the family would notice; for three days the public noticed. The parish priest needs to be seen saying the offices in church (having rung the bell first), giving the needs of the church, the parish and the world full attention.

Fr George Guiver[100] tells us that the history of daily prayer in the Christian Church builds on the tradition of the ancient Judaic practice of daily Temple offering. Sacrifice and prayer were offered, with recitation of the ancient texts. It continued through monasticism and right up to the present day. It was found to be an essential part of the formation of converts to Christianity, as they 'needed simple, urgent formation in the faith if they were to put down roots in this still inchoate body, the Church.' This early discipline was seen very much as part of an attempt to create in converts a sense of belonging. Jesus taught of the one Body and of the branches of the Vine, so ordinary people began to feel very much part of the newly-emerging Early Church in Jerusalem and around the Mediterranean.

The daily prayers of the church had to be led and a minister was appointed to do just that and to tend for the pastoral needs of the community. The psalms were recited regularly and the Lord's Prayer had become firmly entrenched in the minds of converts of the Early Church. 'For the Fathers and medieval Christians the Psalms were a compendium of the gospel, the very words of God through the voice of David, encapsulating the mysteries of Christ.'

Guiver tells us that the clergy joined the people for the daily times of prayer and even with Benedict's guidance, prayer was fairly brief and there was no real expectation of parish clergy to say more than that, with little time allocated for meditation in their daily round of tasks. Guiver, an Anglican monk, also responsible for the formation of ordinands at an Anglican seminary, points to the great amount of time spent by our forebears in meditation. Benedict's own line was that the majority of praying should be done whilst the labour of the day was carried out, wherever that might be. A monk friend has told me that the silence before the morning office enables him to carefully choose a phrase from a psalm to be said and to meditate on it in silence, before using the whole day to return to it as he gives himself to the work of God; as he welcomes visitors to the monastery 'as Christ'[101] he shows them the love of Christ, which underpins his own feeling of Christ's love for him.

For Guiver, the office 'works on a low-key, routine principle, which involves constant return to the same things, the grand themes, the ever-familiar but constantly forgotten laws, the day-to-day face of God.'[102] He also admits that a reading of scripture by rote is not always helpful to the reader, but is fruitful for many. The reading of Scripture in its entirety is something with which religious communities can engage.

But he comes down on the side of shorter passages of scripture being read in order that it may truly 'be the busy Church's sun [...]'[103] drawing on the immense riches of Christian reflection in past and present. By this, he is alluding to the practice of *Lectio Divina*. As an Anglican seminary principal and tutor, he has to balance this with the need to impress on his students the need for careful, lengthy, in-depth study and reading of sacred scripture.

Steven Croft tells us in his book *Ministry in Three Dimensions*[104] that the Apostles in the Early Church were obeying the instructions of Christ and what they were doing through their life of prayer and witness was listening for the Church. He believes that those in diaconal ministry have a ministry of 'waiting for the unfolding of Christ's instructions.' Deacons, priests and later bishops developed a servant ministry and Croft believes that the Church of today needs to do just that through its leadership and membership.

For Croft, much of the work of the parish priest is hidden from view. The priestly function of intercession is the interface between the servant ministry and the acting and interceding on behalf of the people of God. Time spent in personal prayer and public intercession is time spent with God. Those in ministry model themselves on the example of Jesus Christ and of the apostles.

If we seek God, we will seek wisdom. But it was St Paul [1 Corinthians 3:18] who described Christians as 'Fools for Christ' in that 'If you think that you are wise in this age, you should become fools so that you may become wise.' Some ask why we do what we do. Angela Ashwin, in her book *Faith in the Fool*,[105] tells how she answered her son who asked whether it would be far better to serve in a soup kitchen than sitting doing nothing but praying: 'The foolishness of quiet prayer sometimes feels like its main attribute.' It is a 'letting go' of all her preoccupations and thoughts 'in order to be open at a deep level to the inflowing and transforming energy of the divine love.'

We are told by St Paul, in his Letter to the Ephesians [1:3f] that we are destined to be one with Christ, in a personal relationship with him:

> Blessed be the God and Father of our Lord Jesus Christ, who has blessed us in Christ with every spiritual blessing in the heavenly places, just as he chose us in Christ before the foundation of the world to be holy and blameless before him in love.

Andrew Walker[106] thinks that the reason so many clergy have abandoned saying the formal Offices of the Church is possibly that they feel that it has no point: 'its purpose so theoretical as to be meaningless.' It could be that they would prefer something less formal or even do other things with their time, rather than spend time in prayer. The friendship of God is enhanced through this relationship of prayer. 'The daily recitation of the Office may well then be best cast as an integral part of a process of befriending, though both the task and the friendship hallmarked by being useless rather than useful.'

Our relationship with God becomes closer if we return to the word of God and study it and pray through it in love. If we strive through our lives of ministry and witness to bring Christ to the world, it is also likely that there is a high measure of transformation taking place within ourselves. As we seek the love and knowledge of God through our listening to God, our view of others will also change. Jesus Christ in the priest meets Jesus Christ in others.

Enhancing ministry

I believe that it is possible to adapt a monastic rule for use in a parish situation. I believe that the disciplined life which monastic stability can offer, with its regular and maintained rhythm of the various liturgical offices of the Church, accompanied by a regular use of the sacrament of reconciliation and regular (trying to be daily) taking of Holy Communion, can enhance and sustain ministry. The formal prayer contained within the Offices of the Day is rooted in reading of the scriptures and reciting the psalms and canticles. I try to counsel colleagues to do the same, which they would have been accustomed to in their Title (or training) parish and from which they sometimes lapse away.

On my reception as an Oblate of my Benedictine community, I had to agree to make and maintain a Rule of Life for myself, with help from my spiritual director and the Oblate Master. All of the above was included, as well as a commitment to regular amounts of silent prayer and contemplation and a regular (and sometimes guided) study of holy scripture, in order that I might strive to find Christ and to welcome him into my life. For Andrew Walker[107] it is the 'times of silence, thoughts prompted, feelings evoked, contrition and thanksgiving offered, petitions made, intercessions arising' which are all the response to the primary endeavour.

Focused listening, reading and prayer help me see Christ in others, like my monk friend. The words of Christ ring in our ears [Matthew 25:40]: 'Truly I tell you, just as you did it to one of the least of these who are members of my family, you did it to me.'

Endnotes

1. E. Ann Matter. Chapter on *Lectio Divina*, in *The Cambridge Companion to Christian Mysticism. Ed. by* Amy Hollywood and Patricia Z. Beckman. New York. Cambridge University Press. 2012, p. 147.
2. Charles Dumont, OCSO. *Praying the Word of God. The use of 'Lectio Divina'.* Oxford. SLG Press. 1999, pp. 1-16.
3. Pierre Hadot. *Philosophy as a Way of Life.* Oxford. Blackwell. 1995, pp. 101-109.
4. Matter. *Lectio Divina,* pp. 1-16.
5. Michael Casey. *Sacred Reading. The Ancient Art of Lectio Divina.* Ligouri, Missouri. Ligouri/Triumph. 1995, pp. 54ff.
6. Dumont. *Praying the Word of God,* pp.1-16.
7. Matter. *Lectio Divina,* pp.1-150f.
8. Mary Carruthers. *The Craft of Thought: Meditation, Rhetoric and the Making of Images, 400-1200.* Cambridge. Cambridge University Press. 1998, p.1.
9. Rowan Williams. *Silence and Honey Cakes. The wisdom of the desert.* Oxford. Lion Books. 2003, p.11.
10. Jane Tomaine. *St Benedict's Toolbox. The Nuts and Bolts of Everyday Benedictine Living.* Harrisburg USA. Morehouse Publishing. 2015, p.1.
11. St Benedict of Nursia. *The Rule of St Benedict in English.* Collegeville, Minnesota. 1982, p.15(1).
12. Carruthers. *The Craft of Thought,* p.2.
13. Tomaine. *St Benedict's Toolbox.,* pp.32f.
14. E. Glenn Hinson. Chapter on *Baptist and Quaker Spirituality.* In *Christian Spirituality: post-Reformation and Modern. Ed. by* Louis Dupré and Don E. Saliers. British edition. London. SCM Press. 1990, p.332.
15. Sue Pickering. *Spiritual Direction. A Practical Introduction.* Norwich. Canterbury Press. 2008, p.22.

16. John M. Sweeney. *Cloister Talks: Learning from my friends the monks*. Grand Rapids. Brazon Press. 2009, pp.78f.
17. M. Basil Pennington, *Introduced and Ed. Bernard of Clairvaux. A lover teaching the Way of Love. Selected spiritual writings.* New York. New City Press. 1997, pp.112f.
18. Henri J.M. Nouwen. *Here and Now. Living in the Spirit.* London. Darton, Longman & Todd. 1994, p.57.
19. Hadot. *Philosophy*, p.85.
20. Ibid.
21. Carruthers. *The Craft of Thought*, p.2.
22. Carruthers. *The Craft of Thought*, p.4.
23. Robert Davis Hughes III. *The Beloved Dust. Tides of the Spirit in the Christian Life.* London. Continuum. 2008, p.71.
24. Hughes. *Beloved Dust*, pp.71f.
25. A.J Krailsheimer. *Conversion.* London. SCM Press. 1980, p.i.
26. M-B. Said, OSB: *tr. by. Sermons on Conversion [to Clerics], Bernard of Clairvaux.* Kalamazoo, Michigan. Cistercian Publications. 1981, p.31.
27. Hughes. *Beloved Dust*, p.72.
28. F. Bailey Gillespie. *The Dynamics of Religious Conversion. Identity and Transformation.* Birmingham, USA. Religious Education Press. 1991, p.62.
29. Hadot. *Philosophy*, pp.102f.
30. Dom Columba Stewart, OSB, Chapter on *Living the Rule in Community.* (Chapter in Part Four). The Benedictine Handbook. Norwich. The Canterbury Press. 2003, p.279.
31. Julie Kerr. *Life in the Medieval Cloister.* London. Continuum. 2009, p.11
32. Jean Leclercq, OSB. *The Love of Learning and the Desire for God.* New York. Fordham University Press. 1961.
33. St Gregory the Great. *The Book of Pastoral Rule.* New York. St Vladimir's Seminary Press. 2007.
34. Leclercq. *The Love of Learning*, p.13.
35. Leclercq. *The Love of Learning*, pp.191-235.

36. Matter. *Lectio Divina*, p.157.
37. Church of England. *Mission-shaped Church*. London. Church House Publishing. 2004.
38. http://www.freshexpressions.org.uk/guide/examples/mon astic. Accessed 6/5/13.
39. www.contemplativefire.org. Accessed 15/5/13.
40. www.quietgarden.org. Accessed 15/5/13.
41. Rachel M. Shrubas. *Oblation. Meditations on St Benedict's Rule*. Brewster, Mass. Paraclete Press. 2006, pp.xvif.
42. St Benedict. *Rule*. RB59, pp.81f.
43. Benet Tvedten, OSB. *How to be a Monastic and not leave your day job. An invitation to Oblate life*. Brewster, Mass. Paraclete Press. 2006, p.71.
44. Casey. *Sacred Reading*, p.62.
45. Mariano Magrassi, OSB. *Tr. by* Edward Hagman. *Praying the Bible. An introduction to 'Lectio Divina'*. Collegeville, USA. The Liturgical Press. 1988, p.5.
46. Meditation is the intermediate stage between reading and the higher activity of prayer and contemplation. It can be in written form or it can be part of a personal spiritual exercise and practice. There can be an element of private self-examination.
47. Albert Manguel. *A History of Reading*. London. Harper Collins. 1996, pp.28f.
48. Manguel. *History of Reading*, pp.42f.
49. Manguel. *History of Reading*, p.56.
50. Leclercq. *The Love of Learning*, p.21.
51. Andrew Louth. *The Origins of the Christian Mystical Tradition. From Plato to Denys*. Oxford. Clarendon Press. 1981, pp.141ff.
52. Ronald Teske. Chapter on *Augustine's Philosophy of Memory*. in the *Cambridge Companion to Augustine, Edd.* Norman Bretzmann and Eleonore Stump. Cambridge. Cambridge University Press. 2001, pp.148-158.
53. R.S. Pine-Coffin. *Ed.* St Augustine: *Confessions*. Harmands-

worth. Penguin Books. 1961, p.216.

54. Richard P. McBrien, Ed. *Encyclopedia of Catholicism*. New York. Harper Collins. 1995, p.1264.

55. Kenneth Stevenson. *Rooted in Detachment. Living the Transfiguration*. Norwich. The Canterbury Press. 2007, pp.148ff.

56. Stevenson. *Rooted in Detachment*, pp.148f.

57. Ivan Illich. *In the Vineyard of the Text. A Commentary to Hugh's 'Didascalion'*. Chicago. University of Chicago Press. 1993, p.8.fn.3.

58. Beryl Smalley. *The Study of the Bible in the Middle Ages*. Oxford. Basil Blackwell. [1952]. 1983, pp.83f.

59. Ian P. Wei. *Intellectual Culture in Medieval Paris. Theologians and the University, c. 1100-1330*. Cambridge Books Online. http://ebooks.cambridge.org/chapter.jsf?bid=CB0976051184 2108. Accessed 29/5/13.

60. Smalley. *The Study of the Bible*, p.86.

61. R.W. Southern. *Scholastic Humanism and the Unification of Europe. Col.II. The Heroic Age*. Oxford. Blackwell. 2001, p.85.

62. Guigo II. *The Ladder of Monks*. Dublin. Cistercian Publications. 1961.

63. Matter. *Lectio Divina*, p.152.

64. Hadot. *Philosophy*, pp.81f.

65. *Dei Verbum 25* (*vide* Philippians 3:8). Quoted in *Catechism of the Catholic Church*. London. Geoffrey Chapman. 1994, pp.34f.

66. Magrassi. *Praying the Bible*, p.5.

67. Donald B. Cozzens. *The Spirituality of the Diocesan Priest*. Collegeville, Minnesota. 1987, p.84.

68. *Catechism*, p.35.

69. Jeremy Taylor. *The Rule and Exercise of Holy Living*. London. Bell and Daldy. 1857 edn, p.271.

70. Magrassi. *Praying the Bible*, p.5.

71. Meditating in silence on scripture, named in honour of the

contribution to solitary living and prayer by Mother Julian of Norwich, a 14th-Century English Mystic.

72. William Bloom. *The Power of Modern Spirituality. How to live a life of compassion and personal fulfilment.* London. Piatkus. 2011, pp.61ff.

73. Thomas-à-Kempis. *The Imitation of Christ.* [1954]. Harmandsworth. Penguin, p.41.

74. Eugene H. Paterson. *The Contemplative Pastor.* Grand Rapids. Eerdmans. 1989, p.42.

75. Church of England Liturgical Commission. *The Alternative Services Book.* Cambridge. 1980, pp.365ff.

76. Michael Ramsey. *The Christian Priest Today.* London. SPCK. 1972, p.13.

77. Christopher Cocksworth and Rosalind Brown. *Being a Priest Today. Exploring priestly identity.* Norwich. Canterbury Press. 2002, 2006, p.103.

78. Bede Frost. *The Art of Mental Prayer.* London. SPCK. 1950, p.135.

79. Ramsey. *Christian Priest Today.*

80. 'Dear Lord and Father of Mankind', a hymn written by John Whittier. *The New English Hymnal, Ed. by* George Timms (Chair). Norwich. The Canterbury Press. 1986 edn. No.353.

81. E. Glenn Hinson. Chapter on *Baptist and Quaker Spirituality.* In *Christian Spirituality: post-Reformation and Modern. Ed. by* Louis Dupré and Don E. Saliers. 1989. British edition. London. SCM Press. 1990, pp.332ff.

82. J. Brent Bill. *Holy Silence. The Gift of Quaker Spirituality.* Brewster, Mass. Paraclete Press. 2005, p.7.

83. Robert Lawrence Smith. *A Quaker Book of Wisdom. Life Lessons in Simplicity, Service, and Common Sense.* London. Victor Gollanz. 1998, p.26.

84. Martin Laird, OSA. *A Sunlit Absence. Silence, Awareness, and Contemplation.* Oxford. Oxford University Press. 2011, p.3.

85. Graham Turner. *The Power of Silence.* London. Bloomsbury

Press. 2012, p.256.

86. Henri J.M. Nouwen. *Here and Now*, p.63.

87. David Bentley. Chapter on *The Struggle for Silence*. In *Circles of Silence. Explorations in Prayer with Julian Meetings*. Ed. by Robert Llewelyn. London. Darton, Longman & Todd. 1994, p.17

88. Kenneth Leech. *Soul Friend. Spiritual Direction in the Modern World*. London. Darton, Longman & Todd. 1977, pp.179ff.

89. Kenneth Leech. *True Prayer. An Introduction to Christian Spirituality*. London. Sheldon Press. 1980, p.121.

90. *The Shorter Oxford English Dictionary*. Oxford. Oxford University press. 1983, p.1222.

91. The New Monastic movements also regard these special skills as important and as core values. The chapter will explore them, which often coincide with 'traditional' monastic spirituality.

92. Pete Sanders. *First Steps in Counselling. A student's companion to basic introductory course.* 3rd edn. Ross-on-Wye. PCCS Books. 2002, pp.78ff.

93. Martin L. Smith. *The Word is very near you. A Guide to Praying with Scripture*. Cambridge, Mass. Cowley Publications. 1989, p.14.

94. Dale C. Allison, Jr. *The Luminous Duck. Finding God in the Deep, Still Places*. Grand Rapids. Eerdmans. 2006, p.177.

95. Hadot. *Philosophy*, pp.84f.

96. Cozzens. *Spirituality of the Diocesan Priest*, pp.54f.

97. Basil Hume, OSB. *Light in the Lord. Reflections on Priesthood*. Slough. St Paul Publications. 1991, p.113.

98. Church of England. *The Canons of the Church of England*. Sixth Edition. London. Church House Publishing. 2000. Canon B11.2.

99. John Pritchard. *The Life and Work of a Priest*. London. SPCK. 2007, pp.24f.

100. George Guiver, CR. *Company of Voices. Daily Prayer and the*

People of God. London. SPCK. 1988, pp.49f.

101. St Benedict. *Rule.* RB53.1, p.73.
102. Guiver. *Company of Voices,* pp.151ff.
103. Guiver. *Company of Voices,* p.167.
104. Steven Croft. *Ministry in Three Dimensions. Ordination and Leadership in the Local Church.* London. Darton, Longman & Todd. 1999, pp.78f.
105. Angela Ashwin. *Faith in the Fool. Risk and Delight in the Christian Adventure.* London. Darton, Longman & Todd. 2009, p.25.
106. Andrew Walker, *Reading and Friendship.* Unpublished part of doctoral thesis. 2013.
107. Walker. *Reading.*

About the Author

John Draper is an Anglican priest and has served in large, urban parishes in London's East End and in Hampshire. Originally trained as a church musician, a spell as a publisher followed, before a career in finance. He is married with two grown-up daughters and he and his wife have two grand-children. He relaxes through music and water-colour painting and enjoys European travel. He is an honorary Canon of Portsmouth Cathedral.

Circle Books

Circle is a symbol of infinity and unity. It's part of a growing list of imprints, including o-books.net and zero-books.net.

Circle Books aims to publish books in Christian spirituality that are fresh, accessible, and stimulating.

Our books are available in all good English language bookstores worldwide. If you can't find the book on the shelves, then ask your bookstore to order it for you, quoting the ISBN and title. Or, you can order online—all major online retail sites carry our titles.

To see our list of titles, please view www.Circle-Books.com, growing by 80 titles per year.

Authors can learn more about our proposal process by going to our website and clicking on Your Company > Submissions.

We define Christian spirituality as the relationship between the self and its sense of the transcendent or sacred, which issues in literary and artistic expression, community, social activism, and practices. A wide range of disciplines within the field of religious studies can be called upon, including history, narrative studies, philosophy, theology, sociology, and psychology. Interfaith in approach, Circle Books fosters creative dialogue with non-Christian traditions.

And tune into MySpiritRadio.com for our book review radio show, hosted by June-Elleni Laine, where you can listen to authors discussing their books.

MySpiritRadio